Dedicated to all our ambitious friends,

who continue to test their limits.

Hangover Remedies
From Around the World

Which one works best for you?

BEVERAGE DU JOUR™

Hangover Remedies from Around the World

Which one works best for you?

First Edition Paperback

Table of Contents

REMEDY THEORIES

"I feel sorry for people that don't drink, because when they wake up in the morning, that is the best they are going to feel all day."

— Frank Sinatra

Remedy theories are the categories listed below that define common self-treatments meant to relieve specific hangover symptoms. To explore the treatments that are right for you, find the predominant symptom(s) of your hangover in the descriptions below and search for recipes that alleviate those symptoms. An index by remedy theory is also available near the end of this book.

Your personal hangover cure may be a combination of two or more categories, or a mix of recipes and ingredients that alleviate multiple symptoms using one concoction. Everyone suffers differently. Hangovers may differ based on the type of alcohol consumed, by what you have or haven't eaten, or by the humidity in the air. Your hangovers in your 20s may be very different than your hangovers in your 40s. Keep this guide close when drinking and you may find an answer to ease your misery no matter what your ailment.

1. Rehydration and Electrolytes

You are certainly dehydrated after yesterday's antics. These are remedies that hydrate the body and replace lost electrolytes. Alcohol consumption increases urine production and blocks the production of a hormone that helps your body hold on to water, which can cause serious dehydration. Electrolytes, like sodium and potassium, are depleted by consuming alcohol.

Fluids and electrolytes are required by the body to function normally. Vomiting can also contribute to loss of both water and electrolytes. Symptoms of dehydration and electrolyte depletion include:

- Thirst and dry mouth, lips, or eyes
- Dizziness
- Fatigue
- Fever
- Strong-smelling or dark urine

2. Raising Blood Sugar

Alcohol can make your body produce more insulin, resulting in low blood sugar. Alcohol also impairs the hormonal response that helps to regulate blood sugar. Eating most any food can raise your blood sugar. The remedies flagged with this category can raise depleted blood sugar and prevent acidosis. People with diabetes are especially susceptible to high and low blood sugar swings when drinking alcohol. Symptoms of low blood sugar include:

- Nausea
- Hunger
- Fatigue
- Excessive perspiration
- Confusion
- Fainting
- Increased heart rate
- Vomiting
- Blurry vision
- Pale skin
- Abdominal pain
- Convulsions
- Bad attitude / irritability

3. Detoxify, Replenish, and Cleanse

Alcohol is a toxin that the liver must remove, but in the process, it creates acetaldehyde, another toxin, which is often the cause of our discomfort. Alcohol can cause significant reductions in B1 (thiamine), B2 (riboflavin), B3 (niacin), B6, B12, Vitamin C, and critical proteins like cytokine. The remedies in this category are meant to aid our livers in their quest to make us right and return to us those nutrients and proteins that were murdered during our revelry last night.

Toxicity from alcohol can last for hours and it may take several days for the liver to recover from a drinking binge. Alcohol poisoning is a serious condition that can cause brain damage and death. If your symptoms are unusually severe, go to a clinic immediately for specialized care. Symptoms due to toxins in your system and low nutrient levels include:

- Slow breathing
- Low body temperature
- Severe exhaustion
- Fever
- Clammy skin
- Increased heart rate
- Slurred speech
- Memory loss or dementia
- Loss in the sense of touch
- Painful pins and needles
- Joint and muscle aches
- Easy bruising
- Depression and irritability
- Loss of appetite

- Weakness
- Diarrhea
- Yellowing of the skin (jaundice)

4. Kill Pain and Alleviate Congestion

The headache is the poster child of hangovers, but alcohol can also cause inflammation in the gut and joints, resulting in multiple aches and general discomfort. Wine and beer especially contain high levels of histamine, which can result in nasal congestion and trouble breathing.

Remedies for this category are particularly used for aches and pains, including headaches and joint pain caused by inflammation, as well as remedies that help reduce congestion and help unclog airways. Other than using painkillers, rehydration is a key to easing many hangover-related pains as the body is drawing water from itself from wherever it can, including from your brain, to help fight off toxins. Symptoms due to inflammation include:

- Headaches
- Stiffness
- Muscle aches
- Joint aches
- Congestion
- Sore throat
- Puffy or sore eyes
- Belabored breath

5. Prevention Methods

"An ounce of prevention is worth a pound of cure."

—Ben Franklin

Preventing a hangover is far easier than trying to deal with it the next day. Two easy ways to prevent a bad hangover is being well hydrated before you start drinking and to eat before you drink. High-energy foods, especially those rich in B vitamins, have proven to reduce hangover symptoms if consumed before drinking alcohol. If you know you're about to participate in excessive drinking, you have a window of opportunity to plan ahead. There are several options to help prevent a bad hangover before you even start drinking, and a variety of remedies that really do help.

The type of alcohol you consume may determine how you feel the next day. In general, sugary wines, cheap liquors, and candy cocktails are going to take a bigger toll. Also, if you've been out partying, before going to bed, wash your hands and face to get rid of germs that might linger since alcohol may impair your immune system.

6. Magic

> "Magic's just science that we don't understand yet."
>
> —Arthur C. Clarke

Remedies marked with Magic are real methods that some people swear by to fix what ails them, but many are treatments that shouldn't actually work, or at least that have no scientific explanation that we understand…yet.

We do have an idea of what happens regarding two of the most popular magic remedies in this category: 1) Hair of the Dog remedies, and 2) Eating a big greasy breakfast.

Hair of the Dog: A medieval folk remedy for rabies included strapping the hair of the animal that bit you across your wound. The medical philosophy of this course of action can be traced back to ancient Greece. By 16th century Europe, the idea had leant its magic properties to curing hangovers. Sufferers were encouraged to drink a bit of the same alcohol that had caused their hangover. Today we know that drinking more alcohol may postpone hangover symptoms for a short while due to a type of drunken extension, however the symptoms will return, and they will likely last longer than they would have had you abstained from finding that bottle that bit you.

Greasy Breakfast: We have an idea of why this seems to work for many people, (aside from raising blood sugar, which could also be accomplished with so many healthy food choices). Alcohol causes the brain to release galanin, a neurochemical that creates a craving for fatty foods. Satisfying that craving can be pleasurable as far as gaining some relief, and people can interpret any relief as progress. While greasy foods can be a used as a prevention method when eaten before starting to drink, there's no reason a greasy or fatty breakfast should supply relief to any other hangover symptom, except for satisfying that galanin-induced craving. Of course, some people will go back to sleep after eating a big greasy meal, and rest will always help a hangover.

CHAPTER 1

Beverages

"Oh, my God! That is my tooth! Why do you have that? What else is in your pockets?"

— *The Hangover*. Directed by Todd Phillips, Warner Bros. Pictures, 2009.

1)   Coconut Water

Origin: Fiji

Coconut water checks a lot of boxes for whipping a hangover. It offers hydration, electrolytes, and enough sugar to raise your blood sugar (without fructose that could put further strain on your liver).

Recipe: For morning hangovers, start with 16 oz. of coconut water and slowly drink more as necessary.

Remedy theories:

1. Rehydration and electrolytes

2. Raise blood sugar

3. Detoxify, replenish, and cleanse

5. Prevention

2)   Water

Origin: Worldwide

Water is always a good idea not only to help cure a hangover but to prevent them. Three pints of water before going to bed after a drinking binge can go a long way in preventing suffering the next day. If you forgot, drink a pint of water first thing when you wake up.

Recipe: Drink three pints of water before sleeping, or one glass of water with each alcoholic drink. If you already have a hangover, drink one full pint and keep sipping water until you feel human again.

Remedy theories:

1. Rehydration and electrolytes

5. Prevention

3) Himalayan Sea Salt in Water

Origin: Asia

Sodium is an electrolyte that helps the body retain water and pink salt is supposed to contain extra minerals the body may be craving. The citrus adds antioxidants.

Recipe: ·

- 16 oz warm water
- 1 (generous) tablespoon pink Himalayan Sea Salt (for consumption)
- ½ lemon squeezed
- ½ lime squeezed

Remedy theories:

1. Rehydration and electrolytes

3. Detoxify, replenish, and cleanse

4) Vitamin Water®

Origin: North America

Off-the-shelf vitamin water with electrolytes and sugars.

Recipe: Drink 12 oz or more of vitamin water during or after drinking.

Remedy theories:

1. Rehydration and electrolytes

2. Raise blood sugar

3. Detoxify, replenish, and cleanse

5. Prevention

5) Tomato Juice (salted)

Origin: Armenia

It is said that tomato juice can accelerate the rate at which enzymes process alcohol. It also contains electrolytes to keep you hydrated, vitamins to help replenish, and raises blood sugar.

Recipe: Before bedtime, drink 12 oz of tomato juice. Repeat the next day if you still have symptoms.

P.S. add two pickled sheep's eyes and you'll have the Mongolian version of this remedy.

Remedy theories:

1. Rehydration and electrolytes

2. Raise blood sugar

3. Detoxify, replenish, and cleanse

5. Prevention

6)   V8® with Tabasco®

Origin: North America

V8 vegetable juice has many vitamins, electrolytes, and antioxidants to help heal a hangover and offers some rehydration and raises blood sugar. The hot sauce may serve as a distraction to existing aches and pains.

Recipe: 12 oz of V8 with a dash of tabasco.

Remedy theories:

1. Rehydration and electrolytes

2. Raise blood sugar

3. Detoxify, replenish, and cleanse

7)   Soda Water

Origin: China

Soda water (some use Sprite or Ski Soda but soda water seems to work just as well) has been shown to speed up the liver's conversion of acetaldehyde into acetate, implying a shorter hangover duration.

Recipe: Drink 12 oz of soda water before bed and upon waking.

Remedy theories:

3. Detoxify, replenish, and cleanse

8) Bloody Mary

Origin: North America

The Bloody Mary is a 100-year-old cocktail named after Queen Mary I of Scotland, that typically contains vodka, tomato juice, citrus, and a number of spices, herbs, and flavorings. Tomato juice helps protect the liver and contains vitamins and sodium (electrolyte). Any "hair of the dog" drink may delay hangover symptoms for a bit, but ultimately more alcohol will not decrease the damage. Consider a Virgin Mary.

Recipe:

- 2 oz. Vodka
- 8 oz. tomato juice
- lemon or lime squeeze
- pinch of salt and pepper
- celery salt, Worcestershire, hot sauce, horseradish as desired

Stir with celery stick.

Remedy theories:

1. Rehydration and electrolytes

2. Raise blood sugar

3. Detoxify, replenish, and cleanse

6. Magic

9) Virgin Mary

Origin: Britain

Tomato juice helps protect the liver and contains vitamins and sodium (electrolyte). Leaving out the booze is a good idea. Other ingredients are either neutral or slightly helpful in alleviating hangover symptoms

Recipe:

- 8 oz. tomato juice
- lemon or lime squeeze
- pinch of salt and pepper
- celery salt, Worcestershire, hot sauce, horseradish as desired

Stir with celery stick.

Remedy theories:

1. Rehydration and electrolytes

2. Raise blood sugar

3. Detoxify, replenish, and cleanse

10) Bulls Eye

Origin: North America

An egg and juice combo. A raw egg contains cysteine, an amino acid which helps the body break down acetaldehyde. Orange juice contains vitamins A, C, B6, and electrolytes. Freshly squeezed orange juice has more vitamins.

Recipe: Crack a raw egg into 8 ounces of orange juice and think of your happy place while you drink.

Remedy theories:

1. Rehydration and electrolytes

2. Raise blood sugar

3. Detoxify, replenish, and cleanse

11) Bone Broth

Origin: Worldwide

Bone broth is made by simmering bones and meat (chicken, lamb, or beef) to make a stock. Some people drink it for nutritional purposes for many reasons. The water, potassium, and salt content can help rehydrate the body. Glycine content provides antioxidants for inflammation, and broth can raise blood sugar without consuming actual sugar.

Remedy theories:

1. Rehydration and electrolytes

2. Raise blood sugar

3. Detoxify, replenish, and cleanse

12) Coca-Cola®

Origin: North America and Scotland

Coca-Cola was invented as a hangover remedy. In 1886 Pharmacist John Pemberton started giving his patients a combination of caffeine from cola nuts, cocaine, and alcohol, mixed into a thick, sugary syrup, combined with carbonated water. While the painkilling cocaine has been removed, you can still get the blood sugar boost, some hydration, and possibly some gut relief from the carbonation. The Scotland version is called Irn-Bru cola.

Remedy theories:

1. Rehydration and electrolytes

2. Raise blood sugar

4. Kill pain and congestion

13) Cucumber Water

Origin: North America

Cucumber water is mostly water, and any amount of hydration helps. It has a little potassium for boosting electrolytes but otherwise it's the water that is helpful.

Recipe: 3 glasses of cucumber water before bed and/or in the morning.

Remedy theories:

1. Rehydration and electrolytes

14) Beer

Origin: The Netherlands

A good beer is the answer to many things for the Dutch, including hangovers. Beer will raise blood sugar and while the "hair-of-the-dog" cure may delay hangover symptoms for a bit, there is no reason it will help defeat them.

Recipe: Drink a beer.

Remedy theories:

2. Raise blood sugar

6. Magic

15) Kombucha

Kombucha is full of probiotics which are beneficial for the gut and can reduce inflammation, contributing to relief from abdominal pain and nausea. Kombucha is also high in electrolytes.

Recipe: Drink one bottle of kombucha either before drinking, after drinking, or the following morning.

Remedy theories:

1. Rehydration and electrolytes

2. Raise blood sugar

3. Detoxify, replenish, and cleanse

4. Kill pain and congestion

5. Prevention

16) Japanese Raisin Tree (hovenia dulcis) Tea

Origin: China, Japan, and Korea

The tea made from the raisin-like fruit of the Japanese Raisin Tree has been a hangover treatment for centuries. Dihydromyricetin (DHM) is extracted from the Japanese raisin tree for use in pharmaceutical hangover remedies. Its properties are said to speed up the metabolism of toxins and relieve the brain of anxiety.

Remedy theories:

1. Rehydration and electrolytes

3. Detoxify, replenish, and cleanse

4. Kill pain and congestion

17) Rabbit Dung Tea

Origin: North America

A wild west concoction of brewing tea from rabbit droppings. At least they had the hydration part right.

Recipe: Boil some rabbit dung (not recommended).

Remedy theories:

1. Rehydration and electrolytes

6. Magic

18) Green Tea

Origin: Asia

Green tea is a popular home remedy for hangovers in Asia. It can replenish with antioxidants and its catechins protect the liver from excess alcohol.

Recipe: Brew a cup of green tea (2 mins) and sip slowly. Repeat as needed.

Remedy theories:

1. Rehydration and electrolytes

3. Detoxify, replenish, and cleanse

19) Gatorade

Origin: North America

Gatorade provides some sugar and electrolytes that water doesn't have.

Recipe: Steal a Gatorade out of your brother's gym bag and enjoy.

Remedy theories:

1. Rehydration and electrolytes

2. Raise blood sugar

20) Pickle Juice/Brine

Origin: Poland

Pickle juice contains electrolytes including sodium, potassium, and magnesium.

Recipe: Drink one pint of pickle juice and stay near the bathroom.

Remedy theories:

1. Rehydration and electrolytes

21) Herbal Bitters in soda

Origin: Italy

A decent way to raise blood sugar is soda with a kick of bitters. Bitters were created as a digestive remedy and can help settle your stomach.

Recipe: Drink 6 oz of soda with a dash of Angostura bitters and a squeeze of fresh lime juice.

Remedy theories:

1. Rehydration and electrolytes

2. Raise blood sugar

3. Detoxify, replenish, and cleanse

22) Garlic Broth

Origin: Spain, Czech Republic

A potent sick-soup to nourish, rehydrate, and clear congestion. There are many recipes depending on the origin.

Recipe:

- 2 heads of garlic, cloves separated.

- 1 medium potato finely chopped.

- 6 cups chicken broth

- Dried herbs: sage, thyme, parsley, pepper

- 1 cup of tomato juice

- 3 egg yolks

- 4 oz cheddar, or Monterey jack

Simmer all for an hour (except for cheese and eggs). Strain broth. Wisk some broth into egg yolks and pour back into pot. Serve with shredded cheese on top. Add toasted bread if desired.

Remedy theories:

1. Rehydration and electrolytes

2. Raise blood sugar

3. Detoxify, replenish, and cleanse

4. Kill pain and congestion

23) Honey and Lemons in Water

Origin: Worldwide

Honey and lemons help balance blood sugar levels and reduce nausea. Honey has antioxidants and its fructose can prevent the speedy change in the level of alcohol.

Recipe: Dissolve a few teaspoons of honey in warm water. Add the juice of one lemon and drink.

Remedy theories:

1. Rehydration and electrolytes

2. Raise blood sugar

3. Detoxify, replenish, and cleanse

4. Kill pain and congestion

24) Coffee

Origin: Africa

Coffee gets mixed reviews as a remedy. Caffeine will dilate your blood vessels, which may relieve the pressure of an aching headache for a bit. Caffeine may also increase sensitivity to pain and raise blood pressure, so it's best to know your own body's reaction before consuming too much coffee.

Recipe: Drink a cup of coffee. Adding milk and sugar will raise and help balance blood sugars.

Remedy theories:

2. Raise blood sugar

4. Kill pain and congestion

6. Magic

25) Olive Juice

Origin: Europe and Middle East

Like pickle juice, olive juice has electrolytes that aid in hydration. Olives also have antioxidants with anti-inflammatory properties.

Remedy theories:

1. Rehydration and electrolytes

3. Detoxify, replenish, and cleanse

4. Kill pain and congestion

26) Buffalo Milk

Origin: Namibia

The African buffalo milk cocktail contains cream and clotted cream to coat the stomach (and some hair of the dog). More alcohol during a hangover may offer a temporary relief from symptoms but it generally draws the hangover out longer.

Recipe: Mix buffalo cream, clotted cream, and a modest mixture of light and dark rums with a creme liqueur.

Remedy theories:

2. Raise blood sugar

6. Magic

27) Mimosa

Origin: France

A favorite brunch drink, the Mimosa is often a go-to hangover beverage for the morning after. While it does increase blood sugar and provide some vitamins that may have been depleted, any "hair of the dog" drink only delays hangover symptoms for a bit. Ultimately more alcohol will not decrease the damage created by alcohol.

Recipe: Equal parts orange Juice or some other citrus fruit juice and champagne, plus 1/2 teaspoon of sugar.

Remedy theories:

2. Raise blood sugar

6. Magic

28) Protein Shake/Smoothie

Origin: India and North America

Protein shakes and smoothies can replenish lost amino acids and raise blood sugar. Smoothies with antioxidant rich fruits and vegetables can provide additional nutrients and vitamins to combat inflammation and provide relief.

Recipe: Follow instructions for protein shakes or use a tablespoon or two of protein power in your smoothie. Some good choices for smoothie ingredients to fight a hangover include mango, bananas, avocado, kale, spinach, blueberries, oranges, turmeric, pineapple, cayenne pepper, ginger, and coconut water.

Remedy theories:

1. Rehydration and electrolytes

2. Raise blood sugar

3. Detoxify, replenish, and cleanse

4. Kill pain and congestion

29) Red Bull

Origin: North America/Korea

Ginseng is the active ingredient in Red Bull. Studies have found giving ginseng before drinking reduced hangover symptoms. They think that it's because ginseng speeds up alcohol metabolism.

Recipe: Drink a Red Bull the morning after. It should be noted that Red Bull and alcohol together have been known to mask the symptoms of alcohol, often leading to greater intoxication and bigger hangovers the next day.

Remedy theories:

2. Raise blood sugar

3. Detoxify, replenish, and cleanse

30) Pineapple Juice

Origin: Brazil and Hawaii

Pineapple juice contains an enzyme called bromelain, which increases the body's ability to fight pain and reduce swelling.

Recipe: For best results, blend the pineapple into a juice. You can also use canned pineapple if that blender noise is too much to handle.

Remedy theories:

2. Raise blood sugar

4. Kill pain and congestion

31) Tiger's Milk (Leche de Tigre)

Origin: Peru

Tiger's milk is served in Peru as an appetizer, an aphrodisiac, and as a remedy for hangovers. It's a ceviche beverage using raw fish as a base.

Recipe: makes 5 to 6 servings

- 5 oz. white fish (sea bass, sole, and flounder often used)
- 1 cup fish stock
- 1/2 onion
- 3 cloves of garlic
- 2 celery stalks
- 2 cups freshly squeezed lime juice
- 2 teaspoons of freshly grated ginger
- 2 teaspoons of cilantro stems
- 1 teaspoon of aji limo paste
- 2/3 cup water
- 2 and 1/2 teaspoons salt
- 1/3 cup ice cubes

Chop fish and vegetables into small pieces and combine all except for ice into a high-speed blender. Blend for five minutes. Add ice and blend another 30 seconds. Strain and serve over ice. Do not keep in the refrigerator more than 24 hours.

Remedy theories:

1. Rehydration and electrolytes

2. Raise blood sugar

3. Detoxify, replenish, and cleanse

32) Sangrita

Origin: Mexico

The sangrita is a refined sipping chaser for top-shelf tequilas. Not only does its juices complement a good tequila, by drinking a sangrita in tandem with your chilled tequila, you may prevent hangover symptoms.

Recipe: Every bartender makes their sangrita a little differently. To find your own preferred taste, experiment with different levels of sweet and salt by adding or omitting fruit juice or maraschino cherry juice, tomato juice, salt, etc. Serve the following in a separate glass with every two ounces of tequila.

- 1 oz. tomato juice (or Clamato)
- 1 oz orange juice
- ¼ oz lime juice

- 2 drops hot sauce
- 2 drops jugo
- ¼ oz maraschino cherry juice or grenadine (optional)
- 1 small pinch of salt (optional)

Combine ingredients in a cocktail shaker with a small amount of ice, shake, and serve immediately in a two-ounce shot glass. Garnish with tiny lime wedge.

Remedy theories:

1. Rehydration and electrolytes

2. Raise blood sugar

4. Kill pain and congestion

5. Prevention

CHAPTER 2

Food

"You know you're hungover when you brush your teeth with your sunglasses on."

— Anna Kendrick

1) Bananas

Origin: Central America

Bananas contain potassium and sodium to refresh your electrolytes and help stay hydrated.

Recipe: Eat a whole banana before bed. Repeat the next day if still having symptoms.

Remedy theories:

1. Rehydration and clectrolytes

2. Raise blood sugar

2) Pickled Herring

Origin: Netherlands/Germany

Pickled herring is a common remedy in northern Europe and many people pickle their own. Pickled things offer electrolytes, and the fish is said to have several antioxidants.

Recipe: Eat several ounces of pickled herring on its own or with chopped onions on a sandwich.

Remedy theories:

1. Rehydration and electrolytes

2. Raise blood sugar

3. Detoxify, replenish, and cleanse

3) Burned Toast

Origin: Great Britain

Originally thought to have detoxifying qualities because of the char formed when burning, it turns out that the charcoal on burned toast is not active, and so offers no such benefits. It will raise blood sugar though, if not completely charred.

Remedy theories:

2. Raise blood sugar,

6. Magic

4) Sweet Potatoes

Origin: Africa/Central America

Sweet potatoes contain lots of vitamin A, plus electrolytes, magnesium and potassium.

Recipe: Mashed, baked, or fried, your choice.

Remedy theories:

1. Rehydration and electrolytes

2. Raise blood sugar

3. Detoxify, replenish, and cleanse

5) Potassium-rich Foods

Origin: Worldwide

Potassium is an electrolyte that helps the body retain water. Eating potassium-rich foods helps to fight against dehydration and balance body chemistry.

Recipe: Eat foods containing potassium: avocados, bananas, oranges, apricots, grapefruit, honeydew and cantaloupe melon, leafy greens, spinach, broccoli, potatoes, mushrooms, and peas.

Remedy theories:

1. Rehydration and electrolytes

2. Raise blood sugar

5. Prevention

6) Nikolaschka

Origin: Russia

Apparently invented by Czar Nicholas II, this lemon, coffee, and sugar remedy would help raise blood sugar, and provide some antioxidants and liver support.

Recipe: Sprinkle ground coffee and sugar over a slice of lemon and eat it in one bite (then take a shot of vodka as a chaser).

Remedy theories:

2. Raise blood sugar

3. Detoxify, replenish, and cleanse

6. Magic

7) Potatoes

Origin: Ireland

Potatoes have plenty of potassium, an electrolyte that helps you stay hydrated.

Recipe: However you decide to prepare your potatoes, be sure to leave the skins on to get a good dose of potassium.

Remedy theories:

1. Rehydration and electrolytes

2. Raise blood sugar.

8) Sauerkraut

Origin: Eastern Europe

Eating sauerkraut is an ancient hangover remedy that has some merit. It is rich in vitamin C, electrolytes, sodium, and other enzymes, and helps settle the stomach with probiotics.

Recipe: Eat a cup of sauerkraut upon waking with hangover symptoms. May also be used as the main ingredient in a vegetable broth soup.

Remedy theories:

1. Rehydration and electrolytes

2. Raise blood sugar

3. Detoxify, replenish, and cleanse

9) Prairie Oyster

Origin: North America

An old favorite, named for what it looks like (or feels like going down) rather than the ingredients. A raw egg contains cysteine, an amino acid which helps the body break down acetaldehyde, which may be the secret ingredient here. Tomato juice also adds some vitamin B, electrolytes, and antioxidants.

Recipe: One raw egg yolk, a dash of Worcestershire sauce, a dash of hot sauce, a dash of salt, a dash of black pepper, a shot of tomato juice.

Remedy theories:

1. Rehydration and electrolytes

2. Raise blood sugar

3. Detoxify, replenish, and cleanse

10) Quinoa

Origin: Bolivia and Peru

Quinoa is rich in protein and magnesium, which may help fight fatigue and nausea.

Recipe: Cook one serving of quinoa according to directions and eat alone or mix with your favorite ingredients.

Remedy theories:

2. Raise blood sugar

3. Detoxify, replenish, and cleanse

11) Ramen Noodles

Origin: Asia

Like chicken noodle soup in the West, ramen is a common hangover remedy in the East, and for the same reasons, hydrating broth, sodium, and raising blood sugar.

Recipe: Any instant ramen will do. If you make your own ramen from scratch (first of all, kudos to you) it will taste better and will contain better nutrients than the prepackaged variety.

Remedy theories:

1. Rehydration and electrolytes

2. Raise blood sugar

3. Detoxify, replenish, and cleanse

5. Prevention

12) Umeboshi Plums

Origin: Japan

A sour pickled plum including many natural acids thought to aid liver function, calm the stomach, and reduce body aches. The plums also raise blood sugar. Shop for jars with simple ingredients (umeboshi plums, salt, and shiso leaf) that do not contain added corn syrup, sugar, or dyes.

Recipe: Before bedtime, suck on a whole plum until it dissolves and spit out the pit. Repeat the next day if you still have symptoms.

Remedy theories:

2. Raise blood sugar

3. Detoxify, replenish, and cleanse

4. Kill pain and congestion

5. Prevention

13) Rassolnik

Origin: Russia

Rassol is a pickled sauerkraut juice that contains electrolytes.

Recipe: Make a soup from sauerkraut juice. Many people add beef, garlic, and herbs to make this a bit more palatable.

Remedy theories:

1. Rehydration and electrolytes

2. Raise blood sugar

14) Sheep's Head Terrine

Origin: Iceland

Recipe: Start with a whole sheep's head, singe all the hair, and cut the head in half with your battle axe. Boil the 2 halves in salted water. Collect the meat as it comes off the bone. Cool the meat in the fridge or a cool babbling brook until ready to eat.

Remedy theories:

2. Raise blood sugar

6. Magic

15) Charcoal (non-activated)

Origin: Ancient

Humans have used charcoal to settle their stomachs for thousands of years because it does absorb certain poisons in the gut. The jury is still out on what exactly activated charcoal does when you're drinking. For some it appears to delay drunkenness. Others claim it prevents hangover systems. But alcohol does not bind to activated charcoal. It does appear to bind to acetaldehyde and formaldehyde, two components attributed to creating hangovers. Non-activated charcoal, like you find on burnt toast or old campfires, does not have the adsorption properties of activated charcoal, so it's even more of a mystery.

Recipe: Eating a slice of burnt toast or other charred-black foods (not recommended).

Remedy theories:

6. Magic

16) Tiger Toast

Origin: Australia

Vegemite is a spread made from leftover brewer's yeast and tastes like beef bouillon. It is also rich in vitamin B, which is likely the reason some people find relief.

Recipe: Toast a piece of bread. Add butter and vegemite spread. Ad strips of cheese with space in between for the tiger stripes effect. Continue warming in an oven or on the stove to melt the cheese.

Remedy theories:

2. Raise blood sugar

3. Detoxify, replenish, and cleanse

17) Tripe Soup

Origin: Turkey and Poland

Using Honeycomb Tripe (a cow's second stomach) is supposed to be more effective. Tripe is high in vitamin B-12. Tomato paste offers additional antioxidants and vitamin B. The soup will help hydrate and raise blood sugar.

Recipe: Common ingredients include Tripe (up to 3 lbs. in a pot) tomato paste, soup bones, onions, carrots, celery, bay leaves, and salt and pepper. Polish variety calls for allspice and paprika. Turkish recipes add paprika, butter, chili peppers, red wine vinegar, and milk.

Remedy theories:

1. Rehydration and electrolytes

2. Raise blood sugar

3. Detoxify, replenish, and cleanse

18) Avocado

Origin: North America

Avocados are rich in replenishing vitamins and potassium (electrolyte).

Remedy theories:

1. Rehydration and electrolytes

2. Raise blood sugar

3. Detoxify, replenish, and cleanse

19) Avocado Toast

Origin: North America

Avocados are rich in replenishing vitamins and potassium (an electrolyte) and toast is an excellent delivery vehicle.

Recipe: Thinly slice an avocado and lay over fresh toast. Add a little salt.

Remedy theories:

1. Rehydration and electrolytes

2. Raise blood sugar

3. Detoxify, replenish, and cleanse

20) Bacon Sandwich

Origin: England

Bacon sandwiches are a favorite hangover cure in Britain, but it may be that people just like bacon sandwiches and the local pub likes to sell them. You will get a bit of B vitamins from bacon, but most likely it's the umami in the bacon that helps quell a galanin craving.

Recipe: Put some greasy bacon between two slices of bread with cheese. Toasting is optional.

Remedy theories:

2. Raise blood sugar

5. Prevention

6. Magic

21) Poutine

Origin: Canada

Poutine is made with french fries, cheese curd, and gravy. You may never consider eating this mess unless you are drinking or hungover. Alcohol use increases galanin, which in turn increases an appetite for fats. So, there is some chemical satisfaction from that, which may lend a sense of overall relief. But other than raising your blood sugar, there's no reason for excess fats to help your hangover.

Recipe:

- Cut potatoes into fries or bake frozen french fries
- Add chunks of Canadian cheese curd
- Smother plate in a savory gravy
- Add pulled pork (optional)

Remedy theories:

2. Raise blood sugar

6. Magic

22) Cheeseburger & Fries Pizza

Origin: Australia

Pizza, fries, and cheeseburgers all in one bite. Alcohol does increase galanin, which in turn increases an appetite for fats. So, there is some chemical satisfaction from that, which may lend a sense of overall relief. But other than raising your blood sugar, there's no reason for excess fats to help your hangover.

Recipe:

- Roll out and shape pizza dough
- Brush tomato paste and pizza base evenly over dough
- Cover with french fries of choice
- Add grated mozzarella cheese
- Add four cheeseburgers to the top of the pie and add cheese
- Cover burgers with more cheese
- Add Australian bacon and cover with more cheese
- Bake until top is golden brown.

Remedy theories:

2. Raise blood sugar

6. Magic

23) Deep Fried Canary

Origin: Ancient Rome

Piny the Elder mentioned this remedy and it is thought that shutting up the incessant chirps of morning canaries was, for Pliny, like killing two birds with one stone.

Recipe: Remove heads and feathers. Deep fry in oil until done. Chew in silence and consider your life choices.

Remedy theories:

2. Raise blood sugar

6. Magic

24) Crackers

Origin: Europe

Crackers contain fast-acting carbs which will increase blood sugar quickly. Salted crackers like Saltines, Club, or Ritz add sodium to increase electrolytes.

Recipe: Eat a handful of salted crackers with water upon waking.

Remedy theories:

1. Rehydration and electrolytes

2. Raise blood sugar

25) Eggs Benedict

Origin: North America

According to *The New Yorker Magazine*, a Wall Street bigwig named Lemuel Benedict placed a breakfast order at the Waldorf Hotel back in 1894 to fight his hangover. He ordered buttered toast, crisp bacon, two poached eggs, and a hooker of hollandaise sauce. Apart from aiding blood sugar, eggs in any form are good hangovers. They are rich in cysteine, vitamins D and B1, phosphorus, magnesium, iron, selenium, and zinc.

Recipe: Eat some eggs benedict.

Remedy theories:

1. Rehydration and electrolytes

2. Raise blood sugar

3. Detoxify, replenish, and cleanse

26) Owl Eggs

Origin: Italy and Greece

Pliny the Elder recommended 2 owl eggs for a hangover, a remedy which the Greeks already practiced. A raw egg contains cysteine, an amino acid which helps the body break down acetaldehyde. Eggs also contain vitamins D and B1, phosphorus, magnesium, iron, selenium, and zinc.

Recipe: Steal 2 owl eggs (carefully). Swallow them raw.

Remedy theories:

1. Rehydration and electrolytes

2. Raise blood sugar

3. Detoxify, replenish, and cleanse

27) Pickles

Origin: Eastern Europe

Pickle juice contains electrolytes including sodium, potassium, and magnesium.

Remedy theories:

1. Rehydration and electrolytes

2. Raise blood sugar

28) Fertilized Duck Egg with Embryo

Origin: Philippines

The balut egg is the traditional Filipino hangover cure. It is a fertilized duck egg (including the embryo). Chicken and duck eggs contain cysteine, which help break down toxins in the liver. Eggs also contain vitamins D and B1, phosphorus, magnesium, iron, selenium, and zinc.

Recipe: Find a fertilized duck egg and poach it. Put on a blindfold. Go to your happy place. Pretend it's a special custard that the illuminati eat.

Remedy theories:

1. Rehydration and electrolytes

2. Raise blood sugar

3. Detoxify, replenish, and cleanse

29) Fish Scrape

Origin: Peru

Most convenient if you had fish for dinner the night before, fish scrape offers vitamins, minerals, and electrolytes, plus a ginger kick for nausea.

Recipe:

- Fresh lemon juice from 1 lemon
- Fresh lime juice from one lime
- 2 cups of fish stock made from recent fish scraps (floaters are OK and even lucky)
- 1/2-inch grated ginger
- Salt to taste

Remedy theories:

1. Rehydration and electrolytes

2. Raise blood sugar

3. Detoxify, replenish, and cleanse

30) Peppermint

Origin: Europe

Peppermint is said to help with digestion and relieve tension, nausea, detoxification, inflammation, and bloating, all of which can be symptoms of a hangover. Peppermint does contain menthol and analgesic properties, so it may be effective for you.

Recipe: Chew on several fresh peppermint leaves during a hangover or use a teaspoon of dried peppermint to make tea.

As a topical: Add several drops of peppermint oil to warm bathwater. Soak in the bath for 30 minutes, or apply oil to your temples to reduce headaches

Remedy theories:

3. Detoxify, replenish, and cleanse

4. Kill pain and congestion

31) Goulash Soup

Origin: Austria and Hungary

Goulash is a stew made with meat, vegetables, and spices. Paprika is a must (Hungarian if you can find it). Recipes will vary by origin. While goulash will raise your blood sugar and provide rehydration and some electrolytes, it would serve better as a preventative meal.

Recipe:

- 1 large onion chopped
- 1 cup of carrots chopped
- 1/4 stick butter
- 2 tbsp. paprika
- 1 can diced tomatoes
- 2 med potatoes
- 1/4 c flour
- 1 1/2 lbs. stew meat cubed
- 1 tsp. caraway seed
- 2 cups of beef broth

Heat onions in a pot with butter until soft. Add flour and stir. Add other ingredients and stew for 1.5 hours.

Remedy theories:

1. Rehydration and electrolytes

2. Raise blood sugar

5. Prevention

32) Ginger

Origin: Asia

Ginger is used as a natural anti-nausea remedy for hangovers and motion sickness.

Recipe: Ginger can be used in tea form, as a supplement, dried, or candied. Fresh ginger is usually more effective. Try it upon waking if suffering from nausea.

Remedy theories:

2. Raise blood sugar

3. Detoxify, replenish, and cleanse

33) Honey

Origin: Worldwide

Honey can help balance sugar levels and is thought to increase the rate of alcohol elimination.

Recipe: Eat a tablespoon of honey or mix it in with other recipes.

Remedy theories:

2. Raise blood sugar

5. Prevention

34) Honey Sandwich

Raw honey contains antioxidants to help neutralize toxins and its fructose can prevent the speedy change in the level of alcohol. The bread helps raise blood sugar.

Recipe: Put an ample amount of honey between two slices of bread.

Remedy theories:

2. Raise blood sugar

3. Detoxify, replenish, and cleanse

35) Menudo

Origin: Mexico

Using Honeycomb Tripe (a cow's second stomach) is supposed to be more effective. Tripe is high in vitamin B-12. Tomato paste offers additional antioxidants and vitamin B. The soup will help hydrate and raise blood sugar.

Recipe: Common ingredients are Tripe (up to 3 lbs. in a pot) tomato paste, soup bones, onions, carrots, celery, bay leaves, hominy, garlic, and crushed red pepper.

Remedy theories:

1. Rehydration and electrolytes

2. Raise blood sugar

3. Detoxify, replenish, and cleanse

36) Miso Soup

Origin: Japan

Like many salty soups, Miso provides hydration and electrolytes. It also helps replenish vitamin B.

Remedy theories:

1. Rehydration and electrolytes

2. Raise blood sugar

3. Detoxify, replenish, and cleanse

37) Mince and Cheese Pie

Origin: New Zealand

An elaborate and tasty recipe for curing a hangover includes washing down your pie with a glass of chocolate milk (with a pinch of salt). You will gain some rehydration/electrolytes (especially from the milk) and a blood-sugar boost. Greasy foods are only helpful as a prevention method as drinking on a full stomach is much better than on an empty one. The satisfaction of eating fat during a hangover likely comes from an excess of the neurochemical galanin in the brain.

Recipe:

- small, diced onion
- 1 carrot, diced
- 3 cloves of
- 2 cups of beef, minced
- 1 tablespoon Worcestershire sauce
- ½ teaspoon pepper
- 2 cups beef stock
- 1 tablespoon tomato paste
- 2 teaspoons corn flour mixed with ¼ cup water

Cook ingredients a pot for 20 minutes, stirring occasionally. Build your pie using puff pastry as a base, then filling, then 8 slices of cheddar cheese, then puff pastry on top. Bake for 40 minutes at 350 F degrees.

Remedy theories:

1. Rehydration and electrolytes

2. Raise blood sugar

5. Prevention

6. Magic

38) Oatmeal

Origin: Europe

Some argue that complex carbohydrates provide a slow and steady release of sugar into the blood that is best for hangovers. If that's your camp, oatmeal is a good choice. Oatmeal also replenishes proteins and electrolytes.

Recipe:

- 1 cup rolled oats
- 1 cup milk
- 1 cup water
- A dash of salt

Bring liquids to a boil and add oatmeal. Simmer for 3-5 minutes. Add sugar, cinnamon, fruit, or other ingredients as desired.

Remedy theories:

1. Rehydration and electrolytes

2. Raise blood sugar

3. Detoxify, replenish, and cleanse

39) Pho

Origin: Vietnam

Another salty broth soup that cures what ails you. More than hydration and electrolytes, the bone broth soup base includes protein, calcium, and amino acids to help replenish the body.

Recipe: There are numerous pho recipes, but as a rule, make your broth by boiling beef bones (knuckles are popular) for at least an hour. Skim/strain the scum until the broth is clear. Add star anise, onions, garlic, fish sauce, salt, cardamom, ginger, fennel seeds, and cinnamon for that pho flavor. Simmer for another hour and skim again. After that, the other ingredients are up to you. Meat should be cooked sooner. Thinly sliced vegetables and noodles are usually added at the very end.

Remedy theories:

1. Rehydration and electrolytes

2. Raise blood sugar

3. Detoxify, replenish, and cleanse

40) Onion Soup

Origin: France

Onion soup is a hearty remedy that has been around for hundreds of years. The soup aids in hydration with electrolytes, raises blood sugar, and offers some vitamin C. It also helps mask the smell of alcohol on the breath.

Recipe:

- 1/2 cup butter
- 3 tablespoons olive oil
- 5 large Vidalia onions, mandolin sliced
- 2 garlic clove, chopped
- 2 bay leaves
- 2 fresh thyme sprigs
- Salt and black pepper to taste
- 3 tablespoons all-purpose flour
- 1/2 cup dry sherry
- 1 quart beef broth
- 1 quart chicken broth
- 1 day-old baguette sliced
- 1 cup shredded Gruyere cheese

Stir oil, butter, onions, and spices in pot for 10 minutes at medium high heat. Sprinkle flour and add sherry, stir, and wait for boil, add broth then turn to lower heat to simmer for 50 mins. Prepare oven-safe bowls with soup, add a slice of slightly stale bread (add olive oil if desired) cover with shredded cheese and broil for 2 mins or until cheese has melted.

Remedy theories:

1. Rehydration and electrolytes

2. Raise blood sugar

3. Detoxify, replenish, and cleanse

5. Prevention

41) Cayenne Pepper

Origin: French Guiana

Capsaicin found in cayenne pepper has definite pain-relieving properties. It reduces the presence of pain messenger neurotransmitters called "substance P."

Recipe: Add some cayenne pepper to whatever you are eating or drinking to dull a headache or other aches and pains.

Remedy theories:

4. Kill pain and congestion

42) Ginseng

Origin: China

Ginseng has 1,000 uses in folk medicine, but red ginseng has shown benefits in studies for reducing hangovers. It reduces blood ethanol and increases the activity of ADH.

Recipe: Make a from dried red ginseng or take capsules with a full glass of water.

Remedy theories:

1. Rehydration and electrolytes

3. Detoxify, replenish, and cleanse

43) Raw Egg

Origin: Turkey

A raw egg contains cysteine, an amino acid which helps the body break down acetaldehyde as well as many vitamins.

Recipe: Drink it on its own with your favorite additive (not alcohol).

Remedy theories:

1. Rehydration and electrolytes

2. Raise blood sugar

3. Detoxify, replenish, and cleanse

44) Hair of the dog that bit you

Origin: Europe

Alcohol to treat alcohol? It sounds exotic and wise, but it is not a real remedy. What it may do is postpone some hangover symptoms for a few hours.

Recipe: Have a small serving of whatever it was that got you drunk.

Remedy theories:

6. Magic

CHAPTER 3
Other

"I am told by those who know that there are six varieties of hangover—the Broken Compass, the Sewing Machine, the Comet, the Atomic, the Cement Mixer and the Gremlin Boogie, and his manner suggested that he had got them all."

— P G Wodehouse, *The Mating Season*

1) Saline IV Fluids

Origin: North America

Show up to a clinic with a hangover and you're likely to get an IV with Saline solution, commonly containing water for dehydration, sodium (an electrolyte), and dextrose for raising blood sugar.

Recipe: Using IV hydration to fight headaches and nausea is often a quick end for hangovers, depending on the wait in the lobby. There are some urban services that will send a nurse to your door with an IV bag.

Remedy theories:

1. Rehydration and electrolytes

2. Raise blood sugar

2) Rest/Sleep

Origin: Global and Ancient

When in doubt, go back to sleep. A lack of sleep has been shown to increase sensitivity to aches and pains, so sleeping off a hangover likely helps the brain's response to natural painkilling and gives the body more time to self-heal.

Recipe: Go back to bed. At least seven hours of quality sleep after drinking can help heal a hangover. If having trouble going back to sleep, try using binaural beats with Alpha and Theta/Delta waves with headphones (YouTube).

Remedy theories:

4. Kill pain and congestion

3) Vicks

Origin: North America

Vicks VapoRub includes camphor, menthol, and eucalyptus oil, which aid in treating headaches.

Recipe: For a headache, rub Vicks VapoRub on the forehead and temples. Massage in slowly and take deep breaths.

Remedy theories:

4. Kill pain and congestion

4) Yoga

Origin: India

Yoga poses can help stimulate peristalsis, ease pains, and enhance the circulation of lymph to help the body heal itself.

Recipe: There are numerous yoga videos online for hangover-specific poses.

Remedy theories:

3. Detoxify, replenish, and cleanse

4. Kill pain and congestion

5) Sauna

Origin: Finland and Russia

A hot sauna, combined with beating your skin with birch leaves, has been a favorite remedy for hundreds of years. The dry heat causes excess sweating to help detoxify the body, while the leaf beatings are meant to improve circulation (and relieve itchiness due to mosquito bites). Medical professionals warn against further dehydration in saunas, so be sure to stay hydrated.

Recipe: Sit in a hot sauna until satisfactory perspiration is achieved. Have a partner beat you with a branch of birch leaves. If you are alone, flog yourself repeatedly and check to see if people are looking.

Remedy theories:

3. Detoxify, replenish, and cleanse

5. Prevention

6) Voodoo Pins

Origin: Africa and Haiti

A hangover? You must have been cursed by an evil bottle. That bottle responsible must be addressed in the cure, so be prepared to fish through the recycling bin.

Recipe: Recork the bottle(s) that made you sick and stick 13 black-headed pins in the cork (or cap) until your symptoms are gone.

Remedy theories:

6. Magic

7) Marijuana

Marijuana can ease hangover symptoms related to nausea, inflammation, aches, and pains.

Recipe: Use your delivery method of choice. Note that marijuana is not legal in all jurisdictions. Not recommended if you need to drive or operate machinery.

Remedy theories:

3. Detoxify, replenish, and cleanse

4. Kill pain and congestion

8) Vomiting

Origin: North America

If you're freshly drunk and feel like vomiting, you probably should as it could release some of the alcohol in your stomach, but not the morning after. Vomiting after the hangover has begun will do nothing but add to dehydration, because the toxins have already left the stomach and are now in your bloodstream.

Recipe: If you've had too much to drink and feel the urge to vomit, inducing with a finger should not be a chore. Contact a medical professional if you feel very sick right after drinking.

Remedy theories:

3. Detoxify, replenish, and cleanse

9) Booze Bandage

Origin: USA

Booze Bandage is commercial hangover prevention patch containing vitamin B1 (thiamine). B1 is vital for nerve and muscle function and drinking alcohol can cause a lack of thiamine.

Recipe: Before drinking, peel off protectors and place patch on a smooth hair-free portion of skin. Time-release of B1 happens over 8-12 hours.

Remedy theories:

5. Prevention

10) Lemon in your Armpit

Origin: Puerto Rico

One of those cures that we are not smart enough to decipher yet. No doubt that governments are working around the clock as good stewards of your tax dollars to find the scientific logic in this remedy. Some Puerto Ricans swear by it.

Recipe: Cut a lemon into quarters and rub them vigorously under each armpit.

Remedy theories:

6. Magic

11) Wet Sand

Origin: Ireland and Morocco

This remedy involves covering your entire body in sand at the sandy shores of river. While the effect is said to be like having a sauna to leach toxins from the skin, there is little evidence that it should be effective.

Recipe: Have a trustworthy mate bury your body in wet sand for 10 minutes or more the morning after a bender. Watch out for crows and crabs.

Remedy theories:

6. Magic

12) Exercise

Origin: Worldwide

Exercise can release endorphins, which can improve your mood, increase oxygen in the brain, and get the blood flowing to help the body detoxify itself. Professionals caution not to overdo it.

Recipe: Lite exercises include walking, jogging, and stretching. Weightlifting may aggravate a headache.

Remedy theories:

3. Detoxify, replenish, and cleanse

13) Sweat Licking

Origin: North America

A Native American remedy was to run very fast to build up a sweat, then lick the sweat off your body and spit it to the earth (probably more fun as a group). As people with hangovers are often already dehydrated, be sure to hydrate thoroughly when attempting the lick method.

Recipe: Run around to build a sweat, then lick as much of the sweat as possible and spit the salty toxins to the earth.

Remedy theories:

6. Magic

14) Pizzle

Origin: Sicily and China

A pizzle is a bully stick, or to put it bluntly, dried bull penis. Your Sicilian grandfather may tell you they are full of vitamins, proteins, and minerals. They do contain protein, but whether they contain the right vitamins or minerals to fight a hangover is undetermined due to a peculiar lack of research funding. Pizzles are also used for enhancing sexual stamina.

Recipe:

- Step 1. Distract the bull
- Step 2. Just kidding. Don't try this at home.

Remedy theories:

6. Magic

CHAPTER 4

Supplements

"Trust me, you can dance."

— Vodka

1) Zaca® Chewables

Origin: USA, China, and Mexico

An all-natural commercial supplement with antioxidants and amino acids. Active ingredients include Japanese Raisin with enzymes to aid the liver in breaking down alcohol, glutamine for electrolytes and rehydration, prickly pear for vitamin replenishment, and glutathione as an antioxidant and for detoxification.

Recipe: Take 4 chewable tablets before going to bed.

Remedy theories:

1. Rehydration and electrolytes

3. Detoxify, replenish, and cleanse

5. Prevention

2) Activated Charcoal

Origin: Worldwide and Ancient

Activated charcoal comes from burning coconut shells, bamboo, olive pits, and various other substances. As the body cannot absorb charcoal, whatever toxins bind to it are also not absorbed. Activated charcoal that is organic and made from coconut shells is said to be the best option.

Recipe: You can swallow an activated charcoal pill before the festivities, or try making the following cocktail for your first drink:

- 1.5 oz bourbon
- Add a ½ capsule of activated charcoal until it dissolves completely
- .25 oz simple syrup (or dissolve ½ tsp. of sugar in the bourbon)
- .25 oz fresh lime

Shake well with ice and strain into a glass over ice. Garnish with lime wheel.

Remedy theories:

3. Detoxify, replenish, and cleanse

5. Prevention

3) Advocare® Replenish

A commercial juice mix product containing Sustamine®, a patented ingredient that helps rehydrate the body, replace minerals and electrolytes lost. Popular with athletes.

Recipe: Shake or stir contents of 1 stick pack into 355 mL of water. Drink with food and up to 4 times a day.

Remedy theories:

1. Rehydration and electrolytes

2. Raise blood sugar

3. Detoxify, replenish, and cleanse

4) Alka-Seltzer® Hangover Relief

Contains aspirin, sodium, potassium, and caffeine. Do not take with other NSAIDs.

Recipe: Drop the contents of one pouch into 4 oz of water. Drink after dissolving

Remedy theories:

1. Rehydration and electrolytes

4. Kill pain and congestion

5) Dihydromyricetin (DHM)

Origin: Japan

Dihydromyricetin (DHM) is extracted from the Japanese raisin tree (Hovenia Dulcis). It is usually taken as a preventative remedy. Some studies have shown DHM speeds up alcohol metabolism by helping the liver process toxins more efficiently.

Recipe: Take the dose recommended on the product before drinking or before going to bed with water.

Remedy theories:

3. Detoxify, replenish, and cleanse

5. Prevention

6) Emergen-C®

Origin: North America

Emergen-C is a commercial product with a boost of antioxidants and electrolytes. Use the powdered form for hangovers.

Recipe: Dissolve one packet of Emergen-C into club soda upon waking. Some people also add Alka Seltzer.

Remedy theories:

1. Rehydration and electrolytes

3. Detoxify, replenish, and cleanse

7) Cheers Hydrate™

Origin: North America

Commercial capsule product containing a precise ratio of sodium and glucose, meant to deliver maximal osmotic pull into the bloodstream. Includes 1,230 mg of electrolytes per serving.

Recipe: Drink a 12+ oz glass of water mixed with 1 scoop of Hydrate product.

Remedy theories:

1. Rehydration and electrolytes

2. Raise blood sugar

8) Melatonin

Origin: North America

Melatonin is a hormone that helps regulate sleep. Alcohol binges often result in REMless sleep, which adds to the sluggish unrested feeling the next day. Taking the right amount of Melatonin at the right time can help your sleep cycles (but too much or poor timing can make it worse).

Recipe: Take 0.3 milligrams of melatonin 90 mins before going to sleep.

Remedy theories:

5. Prevention

9) Cheers Restore™

Origin: Asia and North America

Commercial capsule product containing a natural extract, DHM (Dihydromyricetin), that reduces irritability and discomfort and increases acetaldehyde metabolism, meant to speed up hangover recoveries.

Recipe: Before sleeping, take 2-4 capsules after your last alcoholic drink with water.

Remedy theories:

3. Detoxify, replenish, and cleanse

5. Prevention

10) No Days Wasted®

Origin: Asia and North America

A DHM detox commercial product used for hangover prevention. Some studies have shown DHM speeds up alcohol metabolism by helping the liver process toxins more efficiently.

Recipe: Take the dose recommended on the product before drinking or before going to bed with water.

Remedy theories:

3. Detoxify, replenish, and cleanse

5. Prevention

11) Advil® (Ibuprofen)

Ibuprofen blocks prostaglandins, which are inflammatory chemical messengers, thus reducing inflammation that causes pain. NSAIDs, like Advil, increase acid in the stomach lining, so if you are sensitive to NSAIDs, use a different method. In fact, the manufacture suggests you don't use Advil at all for hangovers as alcohol can already do damage your stomach lining. Also, never take more than one type of NSAID at a time (aspirin, other ibuprofen drugs, etc.)

Recipe: The manufacturer does not recommend Advil for hangovers. If you are still stubborn about it, please use a low dose.

Remedy theories:

4. Kill pain and congestion

12) Aspirin

Origin: Egypt and Germany

Aspirin's active ingredient: salicylic acid, has been a choice for pain (and hangover) relief for thousands of years, sourced originally from willow bark, jasmine, and other plants. Many hangover headaches are thought to be caused by the increase of acetate in the bloodstream, a result of the body metabolizing toxins. Aspirin blocks prostaglandins, which in turn reduces inflammation and pain. Although aspirin is one of the most common remedies for hangovers, there are risks, as salicylic acid (like alcohol) is also a blood thinner that prevents clotting, as well as a stomach and liver irritant.

Recipe: Take two aspirin (about 650 mg) with a full glass of water upon first waking up. For prevention, take two aspirin immediately before going to bed.

Remedy theories:

4. Kill pain and congestion

5. Prevention

13) Omega 3 Fatty Acids

According to the journal PLOS ONE, Omega-3 fish oil may protect against alcohol-related neuro-damage and the risk of eventual dementia. Whether or not there are any immediate benefits to help cure a hangover is still in question.

Recipe: Take one or more Omega-3 supplements.

Remedy theories:

5. Prevention

6. Magic

15) ZBiotics®

Origin: North America

ZBiotics® is a commercial product that breaks down an alcohol byproduct called acetaldehyde that contributes to hangovers, using good bacteria.

Recipe: Consume one bottle of ZBiotics® before drinking.

Remedy theories:

3. Detoxify, replenish, and cleanse

14) Blowfish

Origin: North America

Blowfish is a commercial tablet product, not to be confused with the poisonous fish of the same name. Each serving contains 500mg of aspirin and 60 mg of pharmaceutical caffeine. Blowfish usually comes with a money back guarantee.

Recipe: Dissolve 2 Blowfish tablets in a full glass of water and drink.

Remedy theories:

1. Rehydration and electrolytes

4. Kill pain and congestion

15) BetterMorning™

Origin: North America

Better Morning commercial capsule ingredients include Dihydromyricetin (DHM) and Alpha Lipoic Acid (ALA) to help detox the blood and ginger for nausea.

Recipe: Take 3 capsules before drinking, 3 capsules before bed, and 3 capsules in the morning.

Remedy theories:

3. Detoxify, replenish, and cleanse

4. Kill pain and congestion

16) Liquid IV® (Hydration Multiplier)

Hydration Multiplier is a commercial non-GMO electrolyte drink mix for hydrating faster and more efficiently than drinking water alone. 1 stick contains three times the electrolytes of traditional sports drinks and has 5 essential vitamins.

Recipe: Dissolve a stick of Hydration Multiplier in a full glass of water and drink.

Remedy theories:

1. Rehydration and electrolytes

3. Detoxify, replenish, and cleanse

17) Antihistamines

Origin: North America

Over-the-counter antihistamines are good for reducing inflammation, which can help congestion, nausea, and certain pains. Some promote further dehydration, so plenty of water should be taken with them.

Recipe: Take the dose recommended on the bottle with plenty of water either before bed or in the morning.

Remedy theories:

4. Kill pain and congestion

18) Dramamine®

Origin: North America

Dramamine is a good choice for seasickness as it can bring relief to motion sickness, dizziness, and nausea, especially if taken as a preventative. If those are your primary hangover systems, then Dramamine may work for you in the same way. It's an antihistamine, which fights inflammation. Note that the drug causes further dehydration, so drink more water.

Recipe: Take Dramamine with plenty of water either before bed or in the morning and then go back to bed.

Remedy theories:

4. Kill pain and congestion

5. Prevention

19) DripDrop®

Origin: North America

DripDrop® is a commercial electrolyte powder invented by a doctor at the Mayo Clinic. It helps hydrate and raise blood sugars.

Recipe: Dissolve a serving of DripDrop powder in a full glass of water and drink.

Remedy theories:

1. Rehydration and electrolytes

2. Raise blood sugar

20) Vitamin B Complex

Origin: Holland

Vitamin B in the body can be diminished with alcohol, especially B1. Studies have shown that supplementing a hangover with B1, B3, and B6 can reduce the severity of a hangover.

Recipe: Take a B complex vitamin, or supplements that include B1, B3, and B6 after drinking, and/or when waking up with a hangover.

Remedy theories:

3. Detoxify, replenish, and cleanse

21) Fleuressence™ by Detox After Party Pack

Origin: North America

The After Party Pack, created by the celebrated partier and drag queen, Detox, contains Milk Thistle for liver health, DHM, prickly pear, and vitamins and minerals including B, C, magnesium, and folate.

Recipe: Drink a full glass of water and take 2 capsules.

Remedy theories:

1. Rehydration and electrolytes

3. Detoxify, replenish, and cleanse

22) Naproxen before bed

Origin: North America

Naproxen is a nonsteroidal anti-inflammatory drug (NSAID) like aspirin and ibuprofen, which reduce inflammation. NSAIDs also increase acid in the stomach lining, so if you are sensitive to NSAIDs, use a different method.

Recipe: Drink a full glass of water and take 2 Naproxen upon waking or take before going to bed as prevention.

Remedy theories:

4. Kill pain and congestion

5. Prevention

23) Milk Thistle

Milk thistle is commonly found in commercial hangover remedies. It is one of the more well-researched treatments for liver disease. Milk thistle acts as an antioxidant by reducing free radical production and lipid peroxidation, has antifibrotic activity and may act as a toxin blockade agent by inhibiting binding of toxins to the hepatocyte cell membrane receptors.

Recipe: Take milk thistle supplements as directed with water.

Remedy theories:

1. Rehydration and electrolytes

3. Detoxify, replenish, and cleanse

24) Lyte Balance Electrolyte Concentrate

Origin: North America

A commercial sports drink high in potassium and magnesium.

Recipe: Drink a bottle of Lyte Balance to replenish electrolytes and aid hydration.

Remedy theories:

1.Rehydration and electrolytes

25) Medi-Lyte®

Origin: North America

A commercial hydration product high in potassium, calcium, and magnesium.

Recipe: Take 2 tablets with a full glass of water.

Remedy theories:

1. Rehydration and electrolytes

Have fun and party safely!

Beverage Du Jour™ contributors:

Todd Hayes

Stacey Howard

Katia Hayes

To help plan your next celebration, visit:

www.beveragedujour.com

GENERAL INDEX

REMEDY THEORY INDEX

1. Rehydration and electrolytes
7,8,9,10,11,12,13,14,15,16,18,19,20,23,24,25,27,28,29,31,32,33,34,36,37,38,39,
40,43,51,52,53,56,57,58,59

2.Raise blood sugar
7,8,9,10,11,12,13,14,15,16,17,18,19,20,23,24,25,26,27,28,29,30,31,32,33,35,36,3
7,38,39,40,43,52,53,57

3. Detoxify, replenish, and cleanse
7,8,9,10,11,13,14,15,16,18,19,23,24,25,26,28,29,32,33,34,35,36,37,38,39,40,44,
45,46,51,52,53,54,55,56,58,59

4. Kill pain and congestion 12,13,15,16,18,27,34,39,43,44

5. Prevention 7,8,9,13,20,24,26,27,29,34,35,37,39,44,45,51,52,53,54,55,57,58

6. Magic 10,12,13,16,17,23,24,27,28,29,30,37,40,44,46,47,55

Hangover Journal

Which one works best for you?

Log your progress below to help you find the right remedy for your hangovers. Different types of alcohols, drinks, and substances may cause different symptoms or require different remedies. Hangover over symptoms may also change with time. Score the effectiveness of each remedy you've tried with (1) being ineffective and (5) being very effective.

The dog(s) that bit me:

Symptoms:

Name of remedy:

Number of hours before drinking or after waking the remedy was used:

Effectiveness score (circle one):   1   2   3   4   5

* * * *

The dog(s) that bit me:

Symptoms:

Name of remedy:

Number of hours before drinking or after waking the remedy was used:

Effectiveness score (circle one):   1   2   3   4   5

The dog(s) that bit me:

Symptoms:

Name of remedy:

Number of hours before drinking or after waking the remedy was used:

Effectiveness score (circle one):   1   2   3   4   5

*   *   *   *

The dog(s) that bit me:

Symptoms:

Name of remedy:

Number of hours before drinking or after waking the remedy was used:

Effectiveness score (circle one):   1   2   3   4   5

*   *   *   *

The dog(s) that bit me:

Symptoms:

Name of remedy:

Number of hours before drinking or after waking the remedy was used:

Effectiveness score (circle one):   1   2   3   4   5

The dog(s) that bit me:

Symptoms:

Name of remedy:

Number of hours before drinking or after waking the remedy was used:

Effectiveness score (circle one):   1   2   3   4   5

*   *   *   *

The dog(s) that bit me:

Symptoms:

Name of remedy:

Number of hours before drinking or after waking the remedy was used:

Effectiveness score (circle one):   1   2   3   4   5

*   *   *   *

The dog(s) that bit me:

Symptoms:

Name of remedy:

Number of hours before drinking or after waking the remedy was used:

Effectiveness score (circle one):   1   2   3   4   5

The dog(s) that bit me:

Symptoms:

Name of remedy:

Number of hours before drinking or after waking the remedy was used:

Effectiveness score (circle one):   1   2   3   4   5

* * * *

The dog(s) that bit me:

Symptoms:

Name of remedy:

Number of hours before drinking or after waking the remedy was used:

Effectiveness score (circle one):   1   2   3   4   5

* * * *

The dog(s) that bit me:

Symptoms.

Name of remedy:

Number of hours before drinking or after waking the remedy was used:

Effectiveness score (circle one):   1   2   3   4   5

The dog(s) that bit me:

Symptoms:

Name of remedy:

Number of hours before drinking or after waking the remedy was used:

Effectiveness score (circle one):   1   2   3   4   5

* * * *

The dog(s) that bit me:

Symptoms:

Name of remedy:

Number of hours before drinking or after waking the remedy was used:

Effectiveness score (circle one):   1   2   3   4   5

* * * *

The dog(s) that bit me:

Symptoms:

Name of remedy:

Number of hours before drinking or after waking the remedy was used:

Effectiveness score (circle one):   1   2   3   4   5

The dog(s) that bit me:

Symptoms:

Name of remedy:

Number of hours before drinking or after waking the remedy was used:

Effectiveness score (circle one):   1   2   3   4   5

*   *   *   *

The dog(s) that bit me:

Symptoms:

Name of remedy:

Number of hours before drinking or after waking the remedy was used:

Effectiveness score (circle one):   1   2   3   4   5

*   *   *   *

The dog(s) that bit me:

Symptoms:

Name of remedy:

Number of hours before drinking or after waking the remedy was used:

Effectiveness score (circle one):   1   2   3   4   5

The dog(s) that bit me:

Symptoms:

Name of remedy:

Number of hours before drinking or after waking the remedy was used:

Effectiveness score (circle one):   1   2   3   4   5

*   *   *   *

The dog(s) that bit me:

Symptoms:

Name of remedy:

Number of hours before drinking or after waking the remedy was used:

Effectiveness score (circle one):   1   2   3   4   5

*   *   *   *

The dog(s) that bit me:

Symptoms:

Name of remedy:

Number of hours before drinking or after waking the remedy was used:

Effectiveness score (circle one):   1   2   3   4   5

The dog(s) that bit me:

Symptoms:

Name of remedy:

Number of hours before drinking or after waking the remedy was used:

Effectiveness score (circle one):　1　2　3　4　5

*　*　*　*

The dog(s) that bit me:

Symptoms:

Name of remedy:

Number of hours before drinking or after waking the remedy was used:

Effectiveness score (circle one):　1　2　3　4　5

*　*　*　*

The dog(s) that bit me:

Symptoms:

Name of remedy:

Number of hours before drinking or after waking the remedy was used:

Effectiveness score (circle one):　1　2　3　4　5

BEVERAGE DU JOUR™

www.ingramcontent.com/pod-product-compliance
Lightning Source LLC
Chambersburg PA
CBHW071020040426
42443CB00007B/861